memory's morning

Also by Anne Blonstein:

the butterflies and the burnings (Dusie Press, 2008)
hairpin loop (Bright Hill Press, 2007)
from eternity to personal pronoun (Gribble Press, 2005)
that those lips had language (Plan B Press, 2005)
worked on screen (Poetry Salzburg, 2005)
the blue pearl (Salt, 2003)
sand.soda.lime (Broken Boulder Press, 2002)

memory's morning

poems 2000-2003

ANNE BLONSTEIN

Shearsman Books
Exeter

First published in the United Kingdom in 2008 by
Shearsman Books Ltd
58 Velwell Road
Exeter EX4 4LD

www.shearsman.com

ISBN 978-1-905700-76-9

Copyright © Anne Blonstein, 2008.

The right of Anne Blonstein to be identified as the author of this work has been asserted by her in accordance with the Copyrights, Designs and Patents Act of 1988. All rights reserved.

Acknowledgements

Grateful acknowledgement is made to the editors of the following publications in which poems from this collection, sometimes in slightly different versions, first appeared: *Blue Unicorn* (gold stone), *Canadian Woman Studies* (ophelia in rotem kleid), *Chase Park* (die gabe der freundschaft), *Colorado Review* (*son corps est un poème jaune*), *Descant* (lashing mauve, yellow games), *European Judaism* (zwischensprachen, die seele meines grossvaters), *Freefall* (green rhythm), *Grain* (die wilde farbe, fin d'une biographie), *Illuminations* (blutungsarbeit + scarlet pimpernel), *Lichen* (graue figur), *Lynx Eye* (nefaire), *Northeast* (nach einer schriftlichen vorlesung), *Notre Dame Review* (CHORUS WITHOUT), *Oasis* (le silence des champs), *Poetry Salzburg Review* (blue spot, *diez rosas de azufre débril, eine geisha mit violetten fächer, a small bit of red over the rim of the snow, wo sich die Wolke niederließ*), *Third Coast* (still life grey ground, . . . ou l'ombrelle verte), *West Wind Review* (strassenfee, zweifelbrücken).

cieletterra, scrimplay, gedächtnisgefängnis, strassenfee, wortschwer and nefaire were published in the chapbook *that those lips had language* (Plan B Press, 2005).

Lemech lebte zweiundachtzig Jahre und zeugte einen Sohn, vier goldene Ringe, aber sie ist in Wirklichkeit nicht, wo sich die Wolke niederließ and *dass der Mensch nicht allein vom Brot lebt* were published in the chapbook *from eternity to personal pronoun* (Gribble Press, 2005).

Contents

lashing mauve	9
Lemech lebte zweiundachtzig Jahre und zeugte einen Sohn	10
cieletterra	11
rhythmus nicht wiederholung	12
la vida verde	13
yellow games	14
blutungsarbeit + scarlet pimpernel	15
fädenfrauen	16
zwischensprachen	17
ophelia in rotem kleid	18
fragmentary blue too	19
ein unvermeidlicher körper	20
scrimplay	21
gedächtnisgefängnis	22
judenkirschen (or 27 hours)	23
tangerine	24
still life grey ground	25
die gabe der freundschaft	26
portrait in green	27
strassenfee	28
blue spot	29
CHORUS WITHOUT	30
und deine Töchter mit dir	34
zweifelbrücken	35
diez rosas de azufre débril	36
vier goldene Ringe	37
eine geisha mit violetten fächer	38
a small bit of red over the rim of the snow	39
wortschwer	40
klangheimlich	41
gold stone	42
die wilde farbe	43
fin d'une biographie (oder memory a mode of thought)	44
nach einer schriftlichen vorlesung	45
zwischen immobilität und bewegung	46

graue figur	47
Wenn eine Frau Nachkommen zur Welt bringt	48
le matin de la mémoire	49
durch die totenlöcher springen	50
nefaire	51
green rhythm	52
vergangenheitvertrieben	53
y el reloj encenizado	54
her silk and saffron retinue	55
die seele meines grossvaters	56
unsinnen	57
Und dann noch bei grauen Himmel	58
aber sie ist in Wirklichkeit nicht	59
wo sich die Wolke niederließ	60
pink lightning	61
asche fällt vom himmel	62
die wolken der venus	63
planet red	64
grey interior I	65
eine hybridstille	66
. . . ou l'ombrelle verte	67
so die Bindung ihrer Seele	68
kassandra in himmelblauen rock	69
lesesaal mit aussicht	70
les oranges sont des athlètes	71
silueta de cenizas	72
le silence des champs	73
die Vorhaut eueres Herzens beschneiden	74
dass der Mensch nicht allein vom Brot lebt	75
das violette band	76
und nichts weiter	77
son corps est un poème jaune	78
grey fireworks	79
dark blue curve	80
blue head-on	81
lemur-orange	82
Notes	85

memory's morning

lashing mauve

evening in january. basel. after coming through a storm of sparks

and hearing musics.
the buried music of orange and blue bracelets on the arm.
jangling wrist to elbow on the arm of a girl whose arm
was blown off by a landmine. the music of churchbells
and of central heating. the songs of lena horne. and
war symphonies. the archives echoing from kabul

to leningrad.
new year greetings. a friend wishes us
ein poetisches one — yes a lyrical one. and she quotes
hans magnus enzensberger on bodies' essential need
for rhyme. my additions : the protein of surprise.
the fat of ommission. and a three queens' cake
with a hidden question.

Lemech lebte zweiundachtzig Jahre
und zeugte einen Sohn
  for t.d.

noah. who would have recognized the scene —
the flooded cellars. the nagging smell
of decomposing rats. the salvage attempts
deep into night's drowned corners.

I'm too old
for this stuff . . . you write. but the rabbis
(more or less) agreed that kabbalah should not be transmitted
to anyone younger than forty : frivolity –
adultery – drunkenness – gluttony – lust –
warfare – the vanities of a boy's world
so some sages said.

and. twenty-one years ago
defying the music of bombs and bullets
his friend celebrated the palestinian poet's
40th birthday

head blazing : "Welcome!
You're no longer a youth."

cieletterra

she discovers sounds that depolarize
her muscles. drumbeats that can stretch
the narrow channels of caution so that night
pours into her taught body. moondanced skin.
shadows digesting silences.

       or is it a forest of piano strings?
a perspexed path. and the scale of walking. in winter.
after orchids. after a conversation between cyanins
some cloud bursts. a migrating when.

notes come giftwrapped in green velvet.
but the fingers that rubbed ghosts
into the cello of her cheek until it squeaked
have bolted the wild door. because she could not
meet her eyes in double graves.

rhythmus nicht wiederholung

dawn chorus on the tram. the sky bleeding black
to the tune of car radios. where does
the blackness flow

now

or then crossing language lines? to the snow.
a prisoner (a murderer) walking through shadows
a trail of red footprints. a baby blue snow that has
fallen from a dream. and could a cherry tree
grow from each footprint their nows might
blossom into polyphors of how to save
the variations in a gene. anticipate.
by rearranging historic sclerosis. inserting
daisies. and transposing a heart's flash. with
the deletable note. not yet deleted. not yet.

la vida verde

x-raged. magically reasonabled imaginings complicating
tomorrowed. the dying walk through me. each one takes
a pearl from my ovaries to pay the ferryman. lead skies
glass skies and broken skies. (this poem is a market
to barter dreams. leave them in the margins
or slip them between sighs and salmon. take away
anything that meets your unexplained.)

                                        because i want to be
buried (not burnt) in a coffin shaped like my memories
lined with a pea-green velvet clad in a dress
of parachute silk stitched with the words
of the suicide poets

                          so the mourners can wear a style
that coats their bodies in roses oceans and stripes.

yellow games

(as sung as : the moon on a quasi-parade across
a moss-framed dream. when you and some
hungerstrikers escape on a diet of feathers. if time
continues while minutes swallow numbers chaos
profundities — those fine roots that ache and pretend
i dances on the outer mouth of its undoing.)

                      as sentimentality dehisces seeds
of alterity. as pomposity leaks from the cities of fear.
as music crumples. the past sends insects and angels
to an incredulous future.

                                          as
mahler's ghost walks through the AIDS ward
of a maternity hospital on a night with too many names
his tears turn to marbles. a black clef in every heart.

blutungsarbeit + scarlet pimpernel
for miriam cahn

dream of a large caged animal half dog half ape
with a long white pelt. the last of its species.
i wanted to hug it. or him. her perhaps. but
had forgotten — human — my germs its susceptibility.
it studied me with large green eyes.

(cellists were playing on three pink videos.
at a peace rally. then the bottom of a shaft
in a diamond mine. screens to memory.)

so write (the eyes asked me) about DNA RNA
chloroplasts mitochondria. i will suckle time
while you synthesize words. love may or may
still correct your misspellt rhymes. but hope
should fall off the ends of your sentences
as god and small cries walk across yellow bridges.

fädenfrauen

*My wife Anna then undertook woman's work;
she would spin wool and take cloth to weave.*

    light projects the weight of colour. but
in the night fey and gaunt dreams infiltrate
the symbols on the bedclothes. she'll not
wash forces and like a kite navigating ground
she dips. sheers. sheathes. then knotting
the corners of imagination's silk-pleated sounds
outsteps us with wings of pink haze. there

is another's nemesis. moontripped on her
ungravity in orbits of burnt kisses brush against
the twisted and spectres released by an eye.
for where do bleached lines lead but to and
through a heartscape of stones.

zwischensprachen

the woman who cannot pronunciate
the dialects of nursery kitchen and home

reads writes

in another scripture attentive to slips.
phraseskin —— the exclusion of others.
if we would call it planet ocean. if we saw
in the sea unnamed colours. if we pulled in
the fishing nets of stones. walked on a beach
of lost stories collecting glassparts. driftwords.
after the war my grandparents went on holiday.
came here to switzerland with my father
and in the alpine trains managed to translate
from strangerness into nearly neighbours : yiddish
and schwyzerdytsch —— two old stories.

ophelia in rotem kleid

colour after death? can memory dance
in shot silk? or must our voices echo in the rafters

of skulls

in smoked romances? you cannot cover
your fear with no choices. superficial
and too deep. dew and rust kiss the surfaces
of a rose petal. the violet tenderness
when you sleep in a silent bed. where
do the crows fly to at midnight? your dreams?
self parables against the grave. fragments
of fear the ellipse. two bodies. two foci. far apart
but touching. at edges. the slow path
of a word chandelier. i stitched this dress
with my blood. those pearls from my ovaries.

fragmentary blue too
after robert frost

veins of it ripped in snow-laden cloudscapes. plastic :
paperclips and whistles. my french dictionary. scraps
of the virgin's robe trapped in pagan cities. a word
so exhausted flunks the symbolic : blue was and blue is and
blue will be. blue : a turquoise the navajos have blessed
born-from-the-sky. my egyptian grammar : those ancients
who descried a difference without naming it : blue as green :
                 cobra
papyrus fresh
               and papyrus written.

    drunk (post-coital) he noted for the artist that :
"It was one of the most pleasurable experiences
I've endured."

                                      as the mountains rise
to extinguish the sun the snow turns from white
to blue. the silence clots. and ice transforms the wet.

ein unvermeidlicher körper

the body that whispers its knowledge familiar in her
rhythms before we touch. a mind that caresses
theorems because i am phasing
skin to air when

the saxophone

stops. love : the bass keeps playing. elegance
& myth. as rhythms reach an ending
their throbbing pursues displacement. blood
superscripted by unbleached song.
when the saxophone returns — time elates into parts.
limbs move to psalms of absence. lips dilate
to the kiss of silence. to the recall of brazen
laughter. a musician renounced one spirit for spirit.
tears came. tender before her time. spanned.

scrimplay

to london. i bring my aunt dark
chocolates and a snow-fringed tiredness. a silent
marrow. a week of uncut dreams. trilingual reels
i have watched or blended me an actor in episodes
projected on the negative side of quiet days.

we discuss the policy of the BBC.
about tapes to keep. serials. interviews.
adaptations. stacks of visual and verbal style.
she asks me (again) : "why do 'people' today
judge the past by present standards?"

i'm reading *the tenant of wildfell hall*.
"they were quite feminist weren't they?"
the three scribbling sisters. like us
childless and critics.

gedächtnisgefängnis

he was born thinking omens.
analysing social learning and habits
with antibodily thoroughness
his mind's high-affinity receptors bind doubt.

talk homes us. mothers absent
in sharing and in life. (fathers alive in shadows
and symbols.) his erudition hones my amorphous
notes. his spiked memory pokes among scented
hopes. a magus among the mannerists he ties
holes in meaning.

i'm attracted to souls that can leak. his
methylates my answers. transcription hesitates.
i want to insert or mutate. replace abstractions
with salt. locks with limpets.

judenkirschen (or 27 hours)

leaving a tradition for more fragile sites.
stretching a telophrase she might bear a curve
elliptically orbit this silence and that word
non-geometry : three axes + one night.

from being dimensioned in emigrating trajectories
to becoming-dermal map — in the folds beneath
an eye she found angels and children dancing on
dissonant pearls : three loops one march.

in a patch of memory she projects a room (walls
painted schoolgirl pink. carpet ash-grey.) for those
who bring a luggage of many languages. and those
homeless in all syntax and grammars. light falls
from a person. not from propositions. breaks
in chalk echoes round three smiles. and one learns.

tangerine
for c.-a.m.

so. perhaps they change colour with the language
of your thoughts : your eyes — velvet brown for english.
blue for french. black for spanish. green frescoes
in the mothertongue that washed and permeated
my softening surfaces.

fa. i imagined schiele
painting us. a brush steeped in tyrian purple
ran with my tongue up your lengthening phallicy. me
he wrapped in a red silk bata placing in my hand
a statuette of the goddess hathor.

la. ravished by syntax. the reception
makes just as much sense as the arrangement. if my i cries
adverbially night has neither prefix nor suffix. your face was
quite. as i buried it in the foldings of my grammar.

still life grey ground

you may write tonight in my red ink. fermented terms.
salted sentences. on skin-thin sheets. begin at an ending
and retranslate it.

                            exilic dreamscape.
a tent in the desert. three people breathing. miriam dances
in her sleep her black hair brushing moses' face. aaron groans
as her knees drum vortexts in his spine.

                                    my fingers
on your pulse. your body reads the lyographies i form
in languages i cannot decipher (her eyes breach rivers
elegizing westward). in my mouth your tongue finds
a speech i was never taught (you interpret disappearance).
the walls of my utterness break — and shed hysteroglyphs.
end at a beginning. reframe it in your want.

die gabe der freundschaft

never an abstraction. even if the gift
is listening. the moon's loneliness
without the stars. a friend cannot think
the conversation. a conversation is
friendship's œstrus.

a friend cannot

control the reception. a friend cannot interrupt
the transfer carries over the role another plays.
based in the other the logorhythm of friendship
is response. (the family might not produce
a friend : leda watching castor and pollux
while helen leaves home.) fate is fixed but not
the destination. impossible to forgo one café
in the archipelago.

portrait in green
for cleaved-abandoned mouths

duchamp's nude trips at the bottom of the stairs — twists
her ankle — and swears

                        her time stretched from egyptian
eyes to that exhausted hue rhyming with you who is not
sitting next to me in the pink straw seat in a riverside café
in spring. in sunshine. in switzerland. under the chink
of coffee cups and beer bottles i hear windows and bones
cracking in cities whose names change each day.

                                    if orgasms
have never been philosophical (but political?) i won't go
to bed then with the men (or women) of isms and ologies.
i will not dream. i'll wake. in the middle of the night. before
dawn. hands growing so strong that the heat lifts my spine
through cries that shatter the dustmites.

strassenfee

under the touch of an alphabet. keep on
keep on going under the compromised heavens
incipient with bats — let the rain wash your dress.
organdie dress. embroidered your ka
on its shoulder straps. keep on dancing
through the ichor spilt onto another road of yearning —
for once upon a time we were fish.

you undergo techniques for adriftness
absorbing a koan. you keep what others garbage
the uncertain conclusions of hearts in pain.
and you let your bare feet run across the caress
of stones. glass. and needles. or this dress

spun
of dreams and electricity.

blue spot

for andrei & ilinka mihailescu

letters let us set up tents of words. guyed by grammar.
galed by gaps between canvas and ground that let
the meanings breathe through. we can be nomads in history
and space collecting magic roots along erratic routes
guided by need. there is no madness in this. nor malady.

                                                 here
words stick to the skin like warts. you cannot rub them off
with soap. or sighs. or scratching. so you wait for them to
sink in. cross the strata of dreaming cells until they slip
between ending and teatime into the blood. when you speak
don't forget —— you absorbed them from the world.

es war zweimal two young men who played with words.
they wanted to rid lessons of repetition. they wanted to be
pun rockers. to startle down the stars.

CHORUS WITHOUT

I
ville malconnue

grey city of strangers. grey city of stranger
than his half-blue poems. inside pink walls

i imagined his walls

the rain offset as dark friend as his voice.
i had piled a dish invoked for ash with foods
as sticky as their names. mouth-fitting.
the foods were also foreign in this hotel
of stains on the street of scholastics. nibbling
aromatics in the language of the dead i could
estimate the bitterest : laughter. and resolve
the lips of the demaligned. the lips of
the living and those of the dead exchange
nightwise. i heard reserved accents
fermenting the walls —: vins revers.

II
près du passé

now i had walked down the long road
he must have walked down countless times to buy

baguettes and german newspapers.

and did the building next to 5 rue de lota
in 1953 house an arab embassy? hope
and a hungry angel limped down the street.
he displaced from empirical flourish to a design
whose form endowed it art. i bought
turkish pastries from a narrow shop
beneath his third home and sought
un crème on *place de mexico.* for a bald man
at the next table i wrote sweeter
than croissants. i knew that my short cut
shocked *les garçons* wanting tables for lunch.

III
entre deux demeures dernières

and one-toned sleep-washed walls like sheets on which
to abstract folds. what word-pigments will time hold?

i could hear him

measuring poems in charcoal in a chilly café
where rhyme crept along a song-baked floor.
because he took monochrome signs
and painted each syllable-leaf in fremder
hues. ground of few roots. unnaturalize.
each blade an unsilenced plea. i was waiting
for night. waiting for music he never heard.
our last nights in that proud city historionic
with stones. bonehand in hand. read as if i
am *du*. death had freed him from pain scores
the lungs of the running. existence bluered.

IV
sur le point mirabeau

i heard a splash. i'd thrown into the water a stone
with a cross as i'd walked over the water.

the cross-bearing stone

was where we still meet. the stone came
from another country. i saw a flute floating
above the water. i saw how her mouthpiece
glittered with loquacity. i saw her notes sticking
to the eiffel tower. i'm eating the past. i'm writing
soundmesh on a bed of echoes. which have
the scents of precision and rupture. i can link
my words to your words to others'. a bridge
is really two bridges. sometimes they meet.
in five dimensions. i saw the flute's shadow
dive.

paris, 16–20 april 2000

und deine Töchter mit dir

mauve for the wildness that freshens
old clothes. blood salts for the taste
of thinking. and ash-washed mouths
to cry this light that crumbles. a boat
from a broken past fishes pause
through the beeswaxed floor. its mast
pierces the moulded ceiling. then

                              you
smoke a lemon cigar contemplating
the incompatibility between life
and numbers.

                between routine
and ritual.

                my fates fill here. chance
and a name (gregarious in solitude).
pouring words and space for scarred
roses into a badly mended bone vase.

zweifelbrücken

"you haven't turned to
religion have you?"

                                                           a child
is folding a letter written by his father
into a heather-blue star. he uses all the imprecision
of the stories sung into his broken cradle. transcription
and modification. translation and interpretation. loops
inserted in twisted copies.

a woman in a faded gingham dress is walking
underneath the balcony when he hangs the star there
for moonlight's kiss. plaster is falling off the walls
of old french châteaux like make-up
washed by tears of guilt from the face
of a textual prostitute.

diez rosas de azufre débril
(after lorca/cohen and others)

and in wien there are ten unfinished memories. a wall
out of which no one might fall. untranslatably. there's a bed
where hair burns between spring and summer. a hand
bleeds on a grey silk dream. and a voice from the future
asks you to take this poem with its wasted womb.

                                     in new york
there's an infinite trattoria where erato waits
on the savants. a hole in the map where doves go to dance
and a soul in the subway dressed in exclamation marks
peddles poems whose kisses dye the lips of time.

                                   in a remote attic
the children may be writing legends with pinions
from a romanian song. while this poem is condensing
behind a mirror of ash.

vier goldene Ringe
 für e.l.-s. am tag der befreiung
 von nationalsozialismus

beth tatooed in a right cheek burns as her walls
are scorched by the tongue looking for a door.
in the other aleph shivers as infinity and zero
meet in a shoreless embrace. blue refrains
leap through the gold loops in future ears
while

      hagar watches the moon rise above desert
edge. she thinks about drowning in the sand
but in her breast a heart dances to the rhythm
of crying children. taking the gold ring from her finger
she throws it further than memory:

                              princess
of a bombdazzled city.

                the unarmed angels
curl up on their hospital cots waiting for morphine
and feather transplants.
last lines we can extend.

eine geisha mit violetten fächer
(for jonas meklas)

kept an urn of words. sealed the lid with passion
and buried it in an uncultivated plot.
as the poet wrote : i am growing old —
the only verb i haven't yet enjoyed.
butterflies with paisley wings fertilize my past.
a white ant dances through its forest of grass.
and the mourner wears her reversible clothes :
the scarlet silks of love. death's carmine velvets.

i savoured a roman voice. it tasted
of claret. silence cannot be interpreted until

it is interrupted. kept a grammar of ash.
scattered syntax with worms. forgot
the title. perhaps the flicker. maybe paper eyes.
or venus and barbie locked in a cold embrace.

a small bit of red over the rim of the snow

the girl slips. from the edge of childhood into
her mother's wedding veil. walks to the garden shed.
in one hand a box filled with an ocean. a rose
(black acrylic) dangles in the other. the air smells
of mustard and chocolate. headphones. a cd. a soft voice
repeating : he can never stop. in a tutu of stockings
(laddered) a dancer flies with moss-eyed bats
into the birches where they roost. followed by death
spurring a horse with eggshell hooves.

                        if there had never been
clouds blue eyes might be less prized. turner
an unknown painter. melancholy a word languishing for
a metaphor

                  or another iceberg broken from dreams.

wortschwer

    the sky sleeps in the pine tree's heartwood.
restlessly. dreaming of storms and immensity.
without being woken by the lessons the tree
recites through her xylem vessels in the night.

                                starked. strengthened by
silence. with each year her leafmouths take longer
opening. having stored their stories now scratch
the air with no more than the greenprints
of death.

    sensitive to the quality of our language the sky
the tree and the river rejoice when ideals remain
photosynthates of our imaginations. figures of
burst and blooming consumed by the rag-eye
they now grow. thinner and thinner.

klangheimlich

      she meets aunts who studied
paralanguages as sensual tutors for difficult
endings. mixed niece. she is a turn in the exit
taking with her the orpimented phrases
eurydice will need to combine with the underworld's
seed.

                                  she does not rejoice
if she does not take into accent the old heaviness.
she mixes the names in a tincture of uncertainty
she paints on her eyelids from canthus to canthus.

    can she dream of a stroke can she dream
that she screams and she screamed useless
useless to return perspective to what she saw
grammar to harmonize cold sweat.

gold stone
for c.m.

decay for beauty. decay for freshness. decay of
the verbs that bind to stiff shadows. decay to the
spirit. decay from the sorrows. time crumbles to parse
through grammatical gauze where their tongues lick
negatives enclosing antimotile bodies. a diamond
dulled by neglect starts to sparkle on a finger at

                    love's edge
tired eyes absorb what chlorophyll does not want.
one self eats cartons of black ice cream. another
sleeps between sheets of apricot sweat. madness.
their reason obeys the fraught of dream. the ache
of music.

                    as the 3-year-old said to her mother :
"now is already yesterday. is today already tomorrow?"

die wilde farbe

a strand of her hair caught

in the moon. it floats. stranded

in the vacuums of language. a dress of
tenderness. a nothing but a sense of decayed.
i love the damaged blossom on the cheeks of
queens caught on the chessboard in a war
between ghosts and dreams. colour. the unworn
pearls while she strings words caught in what
it isn't what it seems. i love the sequence she
reforms what she needs. against all the shine.
when a river reflects into the clouds. a face
cuts in the smoke. a strand of her words
curls like her hair. soft greetings. the daily grind.
a film rejected on gravity. no constants breed.

fin d'une biographie
(oder *memory a mode of thought*)

why when? nail mind to drifting
spaces. a cat astray a

rope of questions. a surprised moon

immune to proper. and where can a rock
buy a mouth to talk to the surf? and where
can a ghost try on the moon's fallen
cheekbones? and where can a buddhist monk
in a time-weft find an accident? all the comets
and all the gongs shame a cold finish. a care
and a scandal of worry. a red place or
maybe september. a kestrel's laugh
at the letter's end. words literally collateral.
i heard a piano piss. saw a whiskey
waiting for a syndrome. i can savour it.

nach einer schriftlichen vorlesung

they are hidden (we are told) in the amazon
forest. in government offices. in our own faces.

the improbability of a single account
is to account for it. they are hidden
(we're telling us) while we cut down
our pasts. those forests. experimenting
in government laboratories. in texts.
bubbles of detergent burst in my sink.
like words. bubbles scoured with silence
that wash the gilt-edged dishes to be
washed again. details rubbing away
and wrist muscles scarred with tiredness.
my hands wipe up all the dissolved nouns.
a tenseness not to break a world without.

zwischen immobilität und bewegung

needle woman stands on the brick cliffs
in clover watching a shadow canter
into the sea. a silent crowd flows around
the exile

and will look back (snow-eyed) into

rose garlands scratched on walls of another
future. without seeing face objectives of art
and public are cleaved by a fault she could
slip a curled hair around. wrecked on sures
of domesticity. suspended in broken corners.
from a tear buried in cement a black butterfly
metamorphoses into her dress. airborne
on the echoes of their boots four old angels
blow butterflies through her open head.

graue figur

(No me conocia nadie) gravity recognized.
associations under grounded rather than signed up
before my gender. resting a spiral of upheavals
in their eyes. the game of response animates
the game of us. escape of the not. give of the real
axes (— fragrances of paradise — ring of wholes —)
by reason advance untidy emotions.

love agonizes in the prison of indifference
windows to the outside curtained by self. not
to speak to each other we speak through screens.
shadows have been swimming through a pool
of disinfected language. but i do not want to bounce
any more

                on the trampoline of their silence.

Wenn eine Frau Nachkommen zur Welt bringt

eating less to carry more. once upon
this mountain word and thing danced a very
amorous risk. so intimate was their embrace so
fast their spinning the audience could not
discriminate

                ecstasy from ellipse.

                                      caught inside
language words are these things. dangerous
as veils around repeating that these

                                          feelings
turned scarlet. damaged the parting lips
of a dream. perhaps the rupture held its breath
in the heartless maturity of every erythrocyte. or
the dilatory energy released from saturated bonds
echoed with rabbinical arguments. her skin
was smooth as jacob's. her name
red like esau's.

le matin de la mémoire

travelling everywhere with the tapestried bag
her mother made

she collects the ends of the future.

she woke this evening in dreams she was dancing
on sky-blue embers whirling with the girls
from the halls of art. she woke on a roof of time.
the structure of the tiles had collapsed
into foreign sounds. lunar winds stroked a page
of dust. for she woke this morning into a red
muslin balldress she may never wear. strapless
for chances. not tamed. nor altered. repaired
hems. in mirror in camera in that helical eye
she danced me. on my ankles hung turquoise
and chillis. rusted cans.

durch die totenlöcher springen

when i was a rabbit living on the inside
of a mimbres bowl

she concentrated on painting me a fur
as thin as the night sky. and as black.
the crescent of my eye germinates
with the moon. supernova nights. no one slept
for twenty-three nights. while the sky performed
an old sun dance. she spat on her paintbrush.
every day left a trace at my foot. they'll bury us.
she with those worn tools of her exacting
the beautiful trade. me with the wrapped bones
of a human. but with ceremony first
they will punch a hole in my chest. collectors
who find my heart : value the lost.

nefaire

    she said that she respected my positions
but she did not understand them. that she
was more attuned to those who cherish
objectives and work toward them. who act
like messiahs.

                last week i wrote to an author
whose paper i had edited asking him
to consider not characterizing mice
as "stupid". he refused.

    on inventing writing humans broke
the cycle of birth death and decay. that written
i put down my pencil pick up a cup of coffee
and scratch an insect bite. immune time.
desires macrophaged in one life
return in dreams. kisses from the
bone.

green rhythm

yesterday's impressions of women dressed in green
as i took my two-hour tramp beside the river.
a german tourist in pistachioed trousers and lime and
lime rope sandals stunned the postcard scene.
her girlfriend a light less bright of oranges. then
as breakably thin as her white hound a friend
in an olive skirt. and every gust of wind came
with a shower of bark. i envy the plane trees shedding
each summer the city's crimes. though i anticipate
the screen of lines. dear sisters . . . will i ever reach the sea?

now — a green plastic bag

                                          on a branch
outside shivering. and the ants the angels and
our ancestors whispering charges against humanity.

vergangenheitvertrieben

      the mouse lemur is having a morning
of doubled dreams. though sleeping alone
she smells smoke through the trees and her ear
still stings from the needletip. she wakes
textwired. shivering.

                                  she knows she's not
like the other wrens. though just as discerning
and promiscuous as her mother and sisters
her tastes exclude blue. but the males. how long
must she suppose for the birth of a red fairy?

      sometimes she is me. and some times you. always
a displaced word. as elusive as the seasilk some call
skin. as the bubbles in spring water. or the magician
multiplying two silences for sound.

y el reloj encenizado

Die Demokratie lebt vom Gespräch nicht von
Schlagwörter und Schlagzeilen. we form the silence
in which the adjective and adverb drown
say the cinders. and reflect the angel's eye across
a constellation of footprints. through taints in the mirror

of separation. and i flowed with the oxygen
with the songs burning in it says the blood. but now
the air chokes me into compositions
your cameras will hide.

                        we flower in the window
boxes of the widows who water the nasturtiums with their
tears say the screams. we have abandoned the mouths
and travel from city to here. from september to the delta.
we are nothing but echoes from censored bodies.

her silk and saffron retinue

gasping with rheumatic eyes. no best-seller. a crack
in the air between loving and living as friends' hands
question around a beating heart of silence. perfume
of burning feathers. late trail of breast milk.
not a dove fluttering in their mouths but the angels
of tomorrow (the messages seeking meaning).
in the shower she rubbed salts and sighs into faults

                              of skin. brainflow? letters
broken from the buried texts. sod ciphers.
the dysfixations of sense. in the shadow of words
neglected danced with miriam on a page peeled off
from a stone. syllables flew with ashes into flax lungs

                                      so
she planted yew trees in these sentences.

die seele meines grossvaters

river. a river beneath another river
of music. the darkest human sounding.

an effort not to fade in airbright blue.

balcony of wood. view of a forest that might
have been painted by the douanier rousseau.
yellow butterfly. a huge pale butterfly lands
on these hands. ripples. recognized. trembling as
the wings turn to paper
then scatter.
a messenger arrives to describe how he died.
(tortured.) how to tell them i have already seen
sulphur and smoke? an office dim with mahogany desk.
an office silent with rattan shadows. his space.
then mine?

unsinnen

my skin. as rippled and dark as water
a soul dived into. the shape of right and that of

respect sparkle like diamond or coal. north sea

or german ocean. my language. it operates. it
cleaves and it cleaves. to beached dreams.
after they crossed the english channel. cuff
linked. lost hearts pinned to their sleeves.
translators absorbed through a gut nursed
in shakespeare. legacy of. to live in a reason
without accents. as if pure maths could solve
unbalanced equations. and as if
applied to. going around as the prickliest pear :
no more passing. as a crow colony nests
in the blastèd oaks.

Und dann noch bei grauen Himmel

yesterdays a poet brought me eyesage and an economist
arrived with a laugh. an artist having already delivered
a mountain lighter than the snow on its peaks.
as black as a lake mirror in a songless country.
and each day i suck a rainbow of sweets — sugarless —
but i have gained the weight of seas. wearing my masks
my flesh my

                              pluralities. satin sentences :
no word can master the silence in an anarchy
of photographs. the fruits that were cultivated
for the flavour of symbols have lost their taste

                              so i pause
between lines with the shadows. not knowing
if the light is being cast by the future or the past.

aber sie ist in Wirklichkeit nicht
    for m.d.g.

—— also an actual meeting ——

                    today
while others celebrate you in a monoculture
of inbred tributes i has slipped into
her poppydress at the edge of two fields
and with an eyelash crosses fragments of dream
with the risk of sentimentality (nostalgia deleted).

here they are precise about the relationship :
doctor-father. here are three blue dahlias. and
a time-sensitive migrant. probing the past
last night she found a sequence in frame
downstream from my name. muted remnants
of your voice. uncoiled. smoky.

                    selfing i
confirms heresy : the acquired inheritance
of affectation. or how we sign our dates.

                        basel 29.viii.2003

wo sich die Wolke niederließ

all i can remember is that i didn't want
the linen tablemats embroidered
with maroon cotton. even as a present.
the reds in my kitchen are bright.
and this morning miriam is walking across the sky.

consider poetic houses and riverboats
and tents. prose roads. too many
asphalt ones. if i cannot "evaluate the future"
perhaps i could try to sustain it
by translating the past with ribosomes
of a rose-scented metabolism. not

                                            to not
break the law of the lazy mouths

where blue waves shear across the page. where
scholars distinguish between effort and work.

pink lightning

inflexible skyscape of a cloudless bay. inflexible
spirit (the angels have fled). inflexible a love
that cannot fog or fade : touch the sea. touch this word
and scratch an orange (with a heart naked as lips
and a haunted eye). seduced from an inflexible
distress one hand played silent keys of a muralled
darkness. the other followed it into folds
of a thigh. inflexible lost to despite and because of

rainbows and monochrome.
pastis and leaves of gold.

if a child is born after her father has died and if
coincidence wears the habits of faith
the reader who has arrived here can lay a wreath
of moons in a cemetery whose gate was locked.

asche fällt vom himmel
for charles lock

our eyes having stretched the frame to the edge of
skies. hands having inserted coffins between
the lines we wind round words silvered hairs. order
and sighs. with soul and knife as wings dreams can fly.
here
      remoted roads bring the student yesterdays : trance.
screen of sea. salt spin of the waves. and a daughter
with granite rocks as shoulder blades walking with
her sisterself in tatters

                                        of stasis.
those skies or the blue wound in philosophy the wild teacher
and angels dive into alone to break the illusion of continuity enter
eyes nostrils mouth ears and skin as lost principles. antigone
is dead. is dead. is dead. but the name's a light-seeking scab.

die wolken der venus

days longer than years. and nights heated by
their conversation. thoughts race around a heart
caught

on the beats of analogy that circulates
fashionwise. and

the sounds of reading refuse to fix echoes on
a coast where the sea kisses shores of darkness.
where an actress turns from call to curve. and
an artist gathers shells and fog. where an arrival
changes her names. near this eaten coast
a bridge of ferns brings a voice as dark as
a forced return to sleeping beauty's barracks.
voice as tall as an abandoned tower. rapunzel
with no hair. in the grey silk dress of a survivor.

planet red

wax-winged and slow-skinned. with a paper heart
on which are written the dreams of the unburied
dead. trash in the garden. form on the sabbath.
who listens stages a quiet opera. restores a temple
where colours heaped with flayed skins form
galleries of desire and forgetting. and walls of detail
sound thinner than morning mist. deeper than decay
though all are as porous as

questions. what to do with the overworked words?
the burnt ones. send them on vacation
or offer them child support? for example — silence.

if names could explode this the telos to reverse a
self silk-legged and night-celled for the suicide scene
needs speech to interrupt loss-enchanted eyes.

grey interior I

— why can't i (always) look straight into the eyes
of the other whose ears must embrace my words?
as if i'll find my thoughts prancing on the motes of dust
— knotted in the wooden table top — flying past
the window in a puzzle of rain. angels fled when we lost
our tongue for their sighs. who can touch no more
the hidden scars in the sky. nor smell the bonds
that decay with betrayal. we might order night like
an espresso whose grains of sugar take a billion years
to dissolve. or tilt it the other way with swirls of cream
we hope won't curdle in our dreams. if lions could talk
(so wittgenstein claimed) we would not understand their

quelps

at the seam of seen.

eine hybridstille
for s.b.

we projected films

which met to form a cold screen between us.
silent

subtitles struggled across contracting air. the border
was nothing but our fears. your menstrual blood.
the border was a borrowed tampon. but
a postponed love. photographs of herselves
surveilled. "the best stories are the ones never told"
of friendship. like this one about a woman
without a history who lined doorless rooms
with yellow dreams. and the woman sick
with a future. bearing to it. herselves unsolved
if we'd disappeared in the other's film. but if i
gifted you a rush of this poem with a hug?

. . . ou l'ombrelle verte

jewel to word. sleep to bone. mouth to coffee. red cross
and white star. work out work out work out. she has no
uncles. at night she sips tea. an essence of critical theory
and hips. her bed floats free from the stalls.
the lovers lost in dreams surprise the telephone. theirs
a free jazz that cannot return to rhythmical lips suspend
bruising notes prelude-like above warm skin. between
her closing eyes. grey approaches. decays inside.

                                           she learns that peplum
is latin for woman's coat. german for epic films.
she revocates the road. walks from thebes through
jerusalem to the cracks of a polar zone. listening
to insects. tasting sea. massaging pain.

                            an old hormonal traveller.

so die Bindung ihrer Seele

it is a story with frayed lips.
like the holes moths digest
in the night. the names
orphans scratch in the bark of a burnt
sky. a morphed trip to the end
of the word.

         not a memory but
a dream washed by arthritic hands.
momentless they pour longing
into commentary. massage chlorophyll
into an arrested neck.

               under
the metaphors the winterheart
can now rehearse contentious songs.
drumming with osteoporotic bones
throw

      her selves into freed adjectives.

kassandra im himmelblauen rock

when one can't halt the ground troops of identity.
selfed. being digested by plaint. later
as a seamstress

to the mouth. selfing. selves. selvaged. a ghost

embroiders a wider method. anguished. along
a noose spun from greek stories. across nerve
gaps stained by theory. her stretched tattoos.
her cork shoes. her turquoise and silver rattle.
self-scened. these excavated fragments
of broken necklaces strung into ungrammared
chains for glossing. pearls from the pure
to the pyred quenching the light in the curves of her
dress : clytemnestra. mother whose curse is song
to those who maintain release might be thong.

lesesaal mit aussicht
for jocelyn

of a garden where the trees are rehearsing
an autumn play. dialogue in another abscisive
language of whispering pigments. a garden
where nietzsche and carl jung

could have strolled with the dead.
shared a picnic lunch

on the scarlet wooden bench. this side
of the glass a tired light flutters onto the table.
sun kisses maat's negative cheek (who
will these law students defend and accuse?).
now three black nuns occupy the bench. a row
of bold ellipses in the shadows of the institutes
of silence. xanthophyll palimpsests
coniferous patience. the red bench is empty.

les oranges sont des athlètes

―― don't fall asleep on the train. so you can't dream
about knotting another in the circle of your desires.
box him into a stolen world of forgetting that
a triangle balances on the tip of ecstasy.

                                      the woman sitting
opposite me with skin as soft as a ripe pear
reading a religious magazine wore shades of clay
and heather. thick tights. sturdy shoes.
and hanging on a silver neckchain a green cross
caught in the hexagonal heart of a *davidsstern*.

                if earthed by facts and winged
by words she is guarded by the angel of colour.
not possible ―― sophie tauber wrote ―― to orthograph
progress. only choices hinder we should not.

silueta de cenizas

caught in a mouth northeast of possibility
lucifer is suffocating in the sounds of without. he came
from the desert. there sand danced on his tongue. but
the mothers he now impregnates bleed broken
chromosomes. and when he claps his hands pins fall out
of their hair. into shapes even the angels no longer recognize.

                        we can lock ourselves
into coffins of tungsten or theories or time but our souls
paint ashes mixed with gunpowder on the walls. scratch
hieroglyphs that anticipate a romantic strike.

                                      on the continuum of meaning
along the asymptote to meaninglessness
from each brake of interpretation
a black bird joins the rabbis.

le silence des champs

bonds between this day of art
and your day's

science. friendship is nothing but
this sadness. friendship is nothing but

this stillness. a breeder i admired walked his eye
through rows of hunch and chance. the human
cannot control the random. the meadow
more and more a desert. or back to marsh.
the biologists who cannot control life therefore
they dissect it. i am no longer there to say
i am seduced by probability. a daughter of
mysteries snared into fractions of a lens.
friendship is more than a statistic. but.
a desire immortalized by memory divides.

die Vorhaut eueres Herzens beschneiden

but colourless green slept furiously.
her dreams had been stolen
by the roar of bombers. laughter
torn out of her memories by marauders.
and even the silence as she crept
behind chiral lips

                    looked like a bicycle
after an accident its wheels spinning the dust
into fidelity.

           because she wanted to entertain
the unquestioned more than the syntagma.
to not praise a masculine pronoun but
to study odd.

                the things don't die. seas can be
poisoned by systems and die. and futures
may die if the breasts of refugees
cannot parse a body's sentences.

dass der Mensch nicht allein vom Brot lebt

contact through the hydrolysis of canvas. as if (as if
not so that) a temperate sea could wear away
these

        pearly feldspars of an island defended by
moths. (and talmudically there are three things
of which one might easily have too much
while a little is good : salt. yeast.
and refusal.)

                she was pericoping when she
took up this feather of language. when she
grasped a hair of blessing. and cut four strings
in a harpsichord of cloud

                         and silence. where
a woman rests on a neon stool
gazing at what was discarded
in the blackwashed refrigerator : bookmarks
and a pale purple halo from the moon.

das violette band
for mela and katharina

women and xerox machines. this was an extreme case
at the cutting edge of locust jaws and seconds.
in an abandoned factory the ghosts of typists
ate angelcakes iced with numbers.

                          wet cells
in xerophyllic bodies frowned. she pressed henbane
on her cheek so she could not speak. she bought a bangle
of pecan shells and silver. time forgot itself in her synthetic
mouth. entering a church of shadows she heard a choir
of silky gurgles : alabaster gulls pierced the parchment roof.

                        we as xenophilic yous
drifting through (the essential). the other friendship lasts
like the laws of a blue sky across which memories
and music roll on truth-composing ellipticals.

und nichts weiter

perhaps as i rode past suburbs quarries
and a misty calm lake i could have imagined
hearing the rumble of human-packed
cattle wagons. the pleas for water ("crème
ohne zucker"). tasted the stench of urine
shit and menstrual blood ("basel. endstation.
bitte alle aussteigen.") but i didn't.

                                        (had
travelled to a ceramics exhibition in yverdon.
reading an essay on sebald's *austerlitz*.)

                                          had
once discovered chance times quietly
poems revise well on trains. the curving
and shadowed windowscapes deform fixed
images. clouddances disorder human syntax

                                              and
their showers disperse what was abstract.

son corps est un poème jaune

do you know the language where the mutations
blossom? shadows bring light into the truth
of sentences? meaning is synthesized
by ribosomes of a dissatisfied metabolism?
the muses scream and the letters seduce?
do you know this language? dancer. and danger.

you know the history with smoke for rafters.
eyes for windows. space with a vase of roses
and broken promises. that shine which things.

in the hannover museums each time the guards
(leaning always in the doorjambs) blinked
i stuck petals back on wilting danish poppies.
gave the dying german girl an antidote for angels.
and stole a kiss from akhenaten's broken lips.

grey fireworks
for t.l.

he wouldn't look into my eyes the actor
with a ragged haircut and muddy boots
embodying one-quarter of hölderlin's kobold
of the line. now restored for intimate theatre
the tower had housed an american library.
would he have borrowed whitman? eliot? h.d.?

      you shouldn't look into my eyes if you're
seeking a sun that rises on the aegean. though
you might find a moon masked in oily vapours.
a north sea. wreckage of last night's conversation.

      it will not look into my eyes. because
the message it will assign must be featherwritten
on skin. arationally. every dream depending
mortally on moments it angeled.

dark blue curve

morning rises on a man at the tramstop. slumped.
a steady trickle of beer falls from his can.
unfermenting dreams. leaking from an oral hand. drop
by drop he slips away from the model on the poster.
as if her glossy bronze skin is too smooth
to support him.

                      yes — tomorrow
in thirsty times the colour of water may indeed haunt
and dismay the indifference.

        the cover of an australian wilderness diary
i had just received depicted (winning shot) bloodwood
trees *(corymba opaca)* against a backdrop of intense
red sandstone. their skinny branches and leaves
trembled (or was it my eyes that were on fire?)

blue head-on
for linda

this pencil did not want to hurt the eyes that would
read its transformations. but tears i was not
saint enough to cry. words i had swallowed
tasting of semen. grey snow. old wallets. if

      you want. the connections come very close.
he did not renege. we have turned to quicker goods.
an art of not finding evil in presence. the vessels sail
and break. tankers. and beer bottles. we have
our democratic institutions. we have
newspapers. (you have television.) antigones
of sophocles hölderlin and brecht. the dying angels
of poetry. and the priceless beauty

                            of others. no. we do not
write by candlelight. but we could.

lemur-orange

. . . and if i vanish through the dawn window
howling. and if a blue tit and angel would escort me
as if hearing the gaps in my harmony. take
my hands. and trace their daunting on this skin.

zilch. serendipity. and who begins their laws.
a refugee paralysed in a lorry's lights might
hallucinate daughters in black dresses
as snowflakes swoon in the skies of andorra
and letter follows word along the precipice — who's
afraid of borders? who's waiting for a rope?

if three women check in at a lakeside promise
imagine them as sisters. as lovers. as friends.
tomorrow they will found a museum to expose
fir cone and tear. the memory of glaciers.

Notes

p. 10   *Lemech lebte zweiundachtzig Jahre und zeugte einen Sohn*
        Genesis 5:28 in the translation by Moses Mendelssohn

p. 16   *My wife Anna then undertook woman's work; she would spin
        wool and take cloth to weave*
        Tobit 2:11

p. 34   *und deine Töchter mit dir*
        from Leviticus 10:14 in the translation by Martin
        Buber and Franz Rosenzweig

p. 36   *diez rosas de azufre débril*
        Federico García Lorca: from *Poeta en Nueva York*

p. 37   *vier goldene Ringe*
        from Exodus 25:12 in the translation by Moses
        Mendelssohn

p. 38   *eine geisha mit violetten fächer*
        Nora Iuga

p. 39   *a small bit of red over the rim of the snow*
        Rebecca Elson: from *A Responsibility to Awe*

p. 44   *memory a mode of thought*
        Rachel Blau DuPlessis: from *Draft 32: Renga*

p. 47   *No me conocia nadie*
        Concha Méndez: from *Canciones de mar y tierra*

p. 48   *Wenn eine Frau Nachkommen zur Welt bringt*
        from Leviticus 12:2 in the translation by Moses
        Mendelssohn

p. 54   *y el reloj encenizado*
        Federico García Lorca: from *Poeta en Nueva York*
        *Die Demokratie lebt von Gespräch nicht von Schlagwörter und
        Schlagzeilen.* [Democracy lives from discussion not from
        slogans and headlines]
        Willi Ritschard

p. 55   *her silk and saffron retinue*
        Estill Pollock

p. 58   Und dann noch bei grauen Himmel
        Hella Santarossa

p. 59   aber sie ist in Wirklichkeit nicht
        from Numbers 5:14 in the translation by Moses
        Mendelssohn

p. 60   wo sich die Wolke niederließ
        from Numbers 9:17 in the translation by Moses
        Mendelssohn

p. 68   so die Bindung ihrer Seele
        from Numbers 30:13 in the translation by Martin
        Buber and Franz Rosenzweig

p. 71   les oranges sont des athlètes
        Hans Arp

p. 72   silueta de cenizas
        Ana Mendieta

p. 74   die Vorhaut eueres Herzens beschneiden
        from Deuteronomy 10:16 in the translation by Moses
        Mendelssohn

p. 75   dass der Mensch nicht allein vom Brot lebt
        from Deuteronomy 8:3 in the translation by Moses
        Mendelssohn

p. 77   und nichts weiter
        from Deuteronomy 5:22 in the translation by Martin
        Buber and Franz Rosenzweig

p. 78   son corps est un poème jaune
        Paul Eluard

www.ingramcontent.com/pod-product-compliance
Lightning Source LLC
Chambersburg PA
CBHW030048100426
42734CB00036B/577